OLD ROYSTON

Photographs and illustrations
selected mainly from Royston Museum's
unique collection

Volume II

Compiled and annotated by
Peter Ketteringham

Preface by
Jane Vincent

Editor:
Norman Gurney

Cortney Publications

ISBN 0 904378 46 2

Published by
CORTNEY PUBLICATIONS
57 Ashwell Street, Ashwell,
Baldock, Herts SG7 5QT

Page Preparation by
Word Design Technology (Clifton)
Printed and Bound by
Henry Ling Ltd, Dorchester

Contents

Caricatures of local personalities by Arthur "Wink" Thair and 1896 extracts from The Royston Crow *appear in various parts of this publication.*

Acknowledgements

In addition to access to the collection of photographs in Royston Museum and the expert help given by the Curator Jane Vincent, we are grateful to have access to the splendid collection of Royston postcards belonging to Jimmy O'Kane.

We are pleased to acknowledge the contributions of the following:

Royston Town Council

Royston & District Local History Society

The Trustees of the Local History Society Collection

Jane Vincent, Curator of Royston Museum and her assistant Carole Kaszak

Robert H. Clark & Son

Warren Bros. & Cooke

Mrs. Dorothy Cooke

Mr. A. Ketteringham

Mr. Peter King

Mr. Mike Lawrence

Mr. Fred Sillence

Mrs. Joan Linwood

Mrs. Bessie Doughton

Mr. J. O'Kane

Mr. H. Shaw

Mr. R. Silver

Royston and District Women's Institute

We are most grateful to Aerofilms of Borehamwood for permission to reproduce aerial photographs of Royston – photographs from their comprehensive collection are available at special prices.

To members of the Thair family we are most appreciative of permission to reproduce cartoons by the late Arthur Thair.

We are also grateful to use extracts from The Royston Crow.

Preface

In 1991, I was lucky enough to have been appointed as Curator of Royston and District Museum, and right from the start, I was impressed by the commitment to Royston's history and heritage by so many local people.

The first Museum that we know about in Royston was the *Royston Institute Museum*. It was built by public subscription, at a cost of £1500.00. The money was raised, and the building was designed and built in the space of a year and it opened in 1856 with a Great Exhibition. The Institute, as it became known, was set up in response to the huge social changes of the nineteenth century, when technological progress required educated workers. It provided a meeting place for adult education, a library and a museum. Lectures were held at night, and Concerts and plays were performed. One of the original curators was Alfred Kingston, who wrote A History of Royston, and many other books on this area. Edward Nunn was also a curator, and amateur archaeologist. In the nineteenth century, the job of curator was often interpreted as the collecting of objects, which were then shoved into cases with little regard to relevance, display or proper care. In fact, the local press reported in 1884 that *'what is known as a Museum, is limited to a few dilapidated specimens of animal life and extremely doubtful identity, with here and there a relic, a glimpse through dusty or broken glass of a mineral or other specimen buried away where it is impossible either to preserve them from decay, or to allow them to be seen.'* Clearly, the principles of good curation were not being practiced, and the management had retreated from the ideals of their years previously.

During this period, photography ceased to become a private hobby for those of a scientific bent, and it became a profession. Many of the photographs in the Royston Museum collection come from this period, and are, indeed, some of the best pictures we possess, for not only do they record scenes or people, but they record them with great clarity.

The Institute was disbanded in 1900. All its assets were handed over to the Local Council. The Council kept the building which is now the Royston Town Hall, but the Library and Museum Collection were sold off and dispersed. The Catalogue of the sale tells us that among the items sold were the tapestry hangings from King James' Palace, and most of the archaeology collection. Many of the specimens were purchased by other Museums, who have in the last few years transferred some of the objects back to Royston. Other items according the account in local papers were sold to collectors abroad.

The Royston and District History society was set up in 1965. Right from the beginning, the members wanted to set up a Museum, and make a collection of items from Royston. Donations soon started to come in. Most unexpectedly, and very touchingly, people came with items from the Institute Museum which had been purchased by their grandparents, and which had been kept for over sixty years in their families, against the day when a new Museum should be started. The Collection soon became too large to be handled comfortably by the individual members of the History Society, and in 1976, a small room in Royston Town Hall was made available by North Hertfordshire District Council. The Museum opened on Saturdays. Manned by volunteers from the Society, it became apparent to the members that they needed professional help. This was given by the North Hertfordshire District Council Museum Service. At all times, the Society did their best to promote good museum practice, and I am very grateful to them for their efforts to document, research and care for the collection.

Nearly another ten years passed, and in 1984, the Society appointed Trustees for the Collection, and entered into negotiations with the Royston Town Council and North Hertfordshire District Council, agreeing on a joint venture to set up a new Museum. The old Congregational Church School Rooms in Lower King Street were rented, and the present Royston Museum was opened in April 1984 by the then Mayor, Mrs. Judy Cresswell, who has maintained her interest and enthusiasm for the Museum. The Trustees, appointed by the History Society sit on the Management Committee with Royston Town Council who run the Museum.

Mr. Peter Ketteringham, who has compiled and captioned the photographs of this book, was one of the many enthusiasts for Royston and its history who founded the Royston and District Local History Society. As one of its honorary Curators, he laid the foundations of good documentation and a proper collection policy. As a Trustee of the Collection he sits on the Management Committee. As a friend of the Museum his contribution cannot be measured. Peter King too, is a Trustee, and he gives many hours of his time every week to the Museum as a volunteer worker and researcher. His contribution cannot be over estimated. His work has been invaluable in helping to assemble the photographs and help with the necessary research for a fairly tight deadline, and his help in tidying up afterwards shows his deep commitment to the museum. Mike Lawrence, too, has helped, and given up his evenings to help in research.

It just remains to thank all who have helped to bring this book to publication. Mr Jimmy O'Kane, who has allowed us to use some of his unique postcard collection of Royston, The Women's Institute whose Golden Jubilee Album has given us two photographs, Mr. Roy Silver who recorded the last day of the old Courthouse (and Harold Shaw who posed as the criminal!), Fred Sillence who freely shares his great love and knowledge of Royston, Sue and Jane, the daughters of Arthur 'Wink' Thair for permission to publish their father's cartoons, and last of all, Norman Gurney the publisher without whose skill and persistence there would have been no book.

Jane Vincent, Curator, Royston and District Museum

Introduction

My first book, Old Royston Vol. 1 was a selection of my favourite photographs from the Museum collection and this selection, which complements that book, is another dip into those archives. Many photos are still in boxes and while it is satisfactory to know they are in safe hands, to put them together in publication means they can be shown to a much wider public.

Some of the photos have dates and information on them, which are easy to process, but I have needed help from a band of Museum volunteers and helpers who have assisted me in solving some of these problems, for which I am very grateful, particularly the Museum Curator, Jane Vincent for her enthusiasm and help. I am especially grateful to my son Richard and my wife for all their help in preparing the photos and captions and their general encouragement.

There are two interesting matters which have been made clear: one is that if Colin Clark continues to take photos, a hundred years of Royston will be recorded by that family. The other item is the enormous number of buildings lost to the town, the excuse being that the roads need to be widened for the motor car. Upon achieving a satisfactory route through the town, we now have a by-pass to take the traffic which makes some of the demolition unnecessary.

I hope browsing through this book will give people pleasure, whether you are new to the town or have happy memories of days gone by.

Peter Ketteringham
Royston, Hertfordshire
October 1995

Publisher's Note

The reception given to the first volume of Old Royston was very encouraging and approving. Whilst this made a second volume appropriate, we have had to be very much aware that our choice would have to be very selective. I believe that this has been achieved, but not with out a great deal of research and heart searching. The finished result, impossible without the active co-operation of so many, is a book with which we can be justly pleased.

Norman J. Gurney
Editor, Cortney Publications

This photo taken about 1914 shows some of the 40 children and 2 of the adults who lived in

errace in Mill Road. It would be interesting to know who they are and where they are now.

1962. Aerial view of Royston, Eastfield Road is bottom centre and the ... ...

1962. Aerial view of Royston. Across the picture is the A10 Royston to Cambridge road looking west. The diagonal road is Garden Walk with Meridian School and its playing fields at the centre. The army camp is bottom left. Before Tesco and the By-pass.

Postmarked August 1906, this panoramic view of Royston was taken from the edge of the Lime Kiln overlooking the cottage gardens in Barkway Road, on a very frosty day.

E arly in the 20th century, most road transport was horse drawn. Gradually at first, but at a faster rate from the 1920's, the internal combustion engine took over from the horse, and the pictures which follow in this section demonstrate the changes up to the late 50's. Since then, of course, the greatest revolution of the 20th century has continued at an even faster pace.

Traffic congestion eventually became utterly intolerable, especially on the main through routes, hence the bypass and the earlier re-routing of the A10.

On this first page of the Transport Section the first picture is of the Bull Hotel with one of the earliest vehicles on the road.

ne Bull Hotel. The covered passage on the left was the main High Street entrance. Large motors
ke the one in the picture often came down from London Road and then did a handbrake turn to
position themselves to go under the arch. Early 20th century.

Above: A very early picture of Stamford's delivery van. The family kept large stables in Stamford Yard, Kneesworth Street (now occupied by a dairy firm). The family lived in a house in front of the yard, which is now a dental surgery. Possibly late 19th century.

Below: Fred Haywood's horsedrawn milk float, delivering fresh milk in Victoria Crescent. The dairy herd was kept in the fields now occupied by Meridian School and Coombelands estate.

Above: The Alderney Dairy was situated in Gower Road. 1930's.

Below: Up to the 1950's T.B. was a killer disease. Tubercular tested milk became very popular and firms offering it soon eclipsed other dairies.

Above: Pedestrian problems outside the Old Palace in Kneesworth Street. This led to the demolition of Duce & Lilly's plumbing and building premises as part of the road-widening scheme.

Below: The difficulties of two-way traffic in Kneesworth Street in the 1950's.

Above: Circa 1930. Mr. Harold Precious hired his charabanc to many groups. This happy company of girl guides are being taken to Aldeburgh.

Below: The '108' Royston to Cambridge bus was a most popular and well-used service. Here it is seen turning into Melbourn Street.

Above: Harold Precious' first garage in Melbourn Road, still run by the same family, now Fina Garage. The bull-nose Morris was for sale at £5 in 1930!

Below: A nasty accident in Baldock Road. (Now the A505.)

Above: Goddard & Dellar's Garage, in Kneesworth Street. Now the site is the John R. Ford garage. Derek Goddard is seen here filling the car of Robert H. Clark III. (late 1950's)

Below: Goddard & Dellar's fleet of vehicles and their drivers on the Heath, mid 1950's.

Logsdon's Garage next to the Manor House Club in Melbourn Street was demolished to mak way for business premises.

A superb caricature by Arthur Thair, well known hairdresser of High Street, whose brilliant dr ings under the pseudonym of 'Wink' appeared in the 1950's. Pictured is Mr. Smith the Pi Tuner using his particular form of transport.

The Silver Link, one of the original Gresley A4 locomotives, passing through Royston station, running-in on the Cambridge-Kings Cross route, a few days before the inauguration of the London- Newcastle four-hour express called *The Silver Jubilee* in September 1935. A most majestic sight.

Melbourn Street in 1913 showing the house on the left as a private house before being tak
over by St. Benedict's Priory. This building together with the others to the Town Hall have
been demolished to make way for the new Police Station and the Health Centre. This w
criticised for losing the old street scene of the town

The Roundabout, Royston.

From Melbourn Street into Melbourn Road. This shows "The Beeches", the home of Dr. anc
Mrs. Fox for many years, which was one of several substantial houses in Royston, which were
demolished to make way for a modern development. This site now has a large block of flats stil
called "The Beeches". (1960's)

The High Street, circa 1900, looking south.

rca 1904, Upper King Street looking south, taken from outside Abbotts Yard looking at W. Horn, otmaker. The notice above the shop reads: W. Horn, Practical hand sewn Bootmaker. Every description of repairs neatly executed.

A 1907 postcard photo of the old railway bridge from Kneesworth Street. The shop on the corner of Queens Road is Bond's the Grocers.

From Kneesworth Street into Old North Road. This is taken from the railway bridge looking north. Ballard's Yard is on the right next to the "North Star" public House. Ballard, amongst other things, was a horse-drawn carrier and contractor.

Two views of Kneesworth Street both before1900:

Above: from the Old Palace, looking towards the Cross. Notice how few shop fronts there are.

Below: The west side looking towards the Cross. The cottages beyond the lady in the long dress were demolished along with "The Crown" public house. Note the decorations of the Conservative Club celebrating Primrose Day 1888!

Two views of The Warren, now the site of the bus station and car park. This was once a thriving little community. Note the above was a Christmas greetings card from the Valentine's series of Souvenir Postcards.

ROYSTON-THE WARREN.

PUB BY ROBERT H CLARK,

Prince of Wales corner where Barkway Street becomes Barkway Road. The pond on the right was one of several drainage ponds in Royston. The Lime Kiln can be seen in the background. The building with the gable end is Wilson, the Carriage-makers. This is a 19th century photograph, one of the earliest in this collection.

London Road, in the cutting looking south (1934). The notice says: Every driver who injures the roadway by descending the hill with a locked wheel which has not a properly adjusted skid pad will be prosecuted by order of Herts C.C.

Archie Gamble ran this shop on the corner of High Street and John Street very successfully for 30 years or more in spite of there being two other large ironmongers in the town.

High Street. Bishops, complete house furnishers and upholsterers. A splendid family-run business established in 1853 and lasted nearly 100 year. Sold to Cambridge Co-op in 19.. Eventually this and other buildings were demolished to make way for Angel Pavement.

ll four photos on this page were taken in the 1950's as part of Royston Urban District Council's ırvey of the High Street, when a photograph was taken of every shop and premises on High :reet. They were taken by Robert H. Clark and the *top left-hand picture* shows young Bob Clark III utside the Gas Office and Showroom. The open door to the left of the Herts & Beds Bacon Factory `as the entrance to Mr. Butler, the dreaded dentist. Generations of schoolchildren from Queens oad School know all about that. *The top right-hand picture:* Apart from change of shop owners this cene on High Street is still there, Royston had quite a number of fine buildings such as this and it a pity so many have been lost. The *bottom left-hand* picture shows Ernie Roberts' shop, Ladies and ents outfitters and Haberdashery, who took over from Moore's after the second world war, riginally Varcoe Grose. A. E. Baker & Co another Royston Grocer *bottom right*. In the 1950's seven grocers ran profitable and well-used shops.

On the left is a 1930's pictu of Titchmarsh's Shop in t High Street which closed la in that decade. Below, what became in the 1950's – Employment Exchang During the war, it was used a government office. Th Exchange was eventual demolished to make way f the extension of Woolworth,

Halstead & Kestell on Market Hill – ironmongers who sold everything from guns to beds. It is now Royston Home Improvement Centre. And below is the Bed Department (c. 1890).

Kneesworth Street. The three cottages are now Ketteringhams, "Fantasia" and a Hairdressers. T[...] shop on the right foreground was a shoe repairers, Mr. Spence.

Below: The cottages have been transformed, and this 1969 photograph shows Ketteringham's, a[...] part of "Fantasia". Some of the building was used by the kennel boys in King James' time.

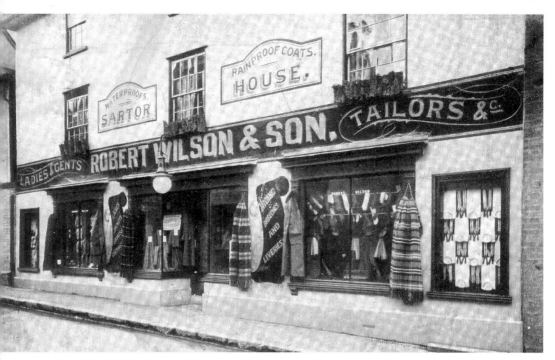

Robert Wilson & Son, later to become Wilson, Son & Randall, Kneesworth Street. They had a large skilled staff to cut and make clothes on the premises. They used all three floors of the building. The shop front is still intact nearly 90 years later. (1907)

Below is a rare photo showing part of the inside of the above shop at the turn of the century.

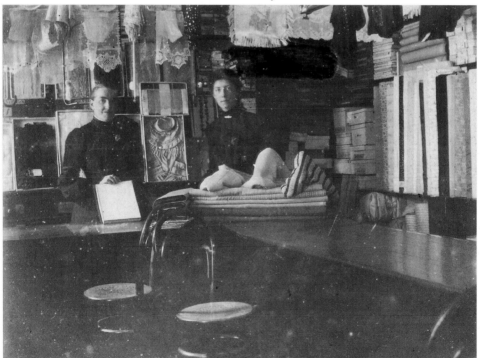

Kneesworth Street from the Cross showing the London Central Meat Co. During the war Mr. Dimmock was manager and errand boys were much in evidence. Friday was the night for making sausages made on a hand machine. This was an important job for a schoolboy of 13 and I was one of them earning 17/6 a week! (Peter Ketteringham).

afts china shop: next door was Crafts Bakery on Fish Hill. The bakery still exists as Days of hwell. After World War II it became the architectural practice of A. Whydale, brother to E. H. Whydale the artist. It is now an Estate Agents.

SIR CECIL NEWMAN SENDING FIRST TELEGRAM.

The first telegram sent from the new Post Office, by Sir Cecil Newman in 1936. The post office was purpose-built in the centre of Royston in Baldock Street in 1936. It served the people of Royston for over 50 years. It was a great shock when it was closed in 1995.

Tommy Danes's Butcher shop. This stood at the Sun Hill end of King Street.
He was noted for his pork sausages, and his bawdy stories.

This site had just been cleared for Royston Bus Station. The large building with the tall chimn
was Jimmy Course's optical lens factory. Some of the instruments used can be seen in Roys
Museum. During World War II parachutes were made here and it was also a blouse factory af
the War.

Polly Dobbin was a great collector of bits of wood and lumps of coal. She was a well known sight in Royston with her box on pram wheels drawn here by 'Wink' Thair.

"Barmy" Matthews: he inherited his father's Chemist and Wine Merchant's Shop in the High Street during the earlier part of this century. After his mother died, he became a recluse, is reputed to have never washed or changed his clothes for 30 years, until he died in the 1940's. His shop was similarly neglected!

NOW IS THE TIME TO HATCH.

JOSEPH PIGG,

Mill Road, ROYSTON,

From *The Royston Crow* 1896.

Royston Market

Part of Nash, Son & Rowley's Sale Yard: On this particular day, Wednesday August 16th 1939 862 lots of fruit were disposed of in addition to other agricultural produce such as poultry, eggs, etc., which in all made a grand total of 1355 lots.

Nash, Son & Rowley also had a cattle market on Wednesdays. The photo below shows a bullock being returned to its pen after a dash for freedom.

bove: Entrance to Willy Stephenson's racing Stables in Upper King Street. On the right is the barn, now a Day Centre. The site is now occupied by Kings House sheltered housing.

elow: Before he took up training, Willy Stephenson was a successful jockey, often riding in the clours of King George V. He came to Royston in 1946. He is shown below with a stable lad. Willy is on the left.

TWO GREAT WINNERS

Above: There was great excitement in Royston when "Arctic Prince" won the Derby in 1951. T[
picture shows Royston jockey Charlie Spares, trainer Willy Stephenson and his wife and the hor[
being led in by Jack Knott, employed at the stables.

Below: "Oxo" trained at Royston by Willy Stephenson won the Grand National in 1959; the jock[
was M. Scudamore.

A once familiar sight on Heath Avenue, the stable jockeys returning from exercising the horses onthe Heath.

Willy Stephenson's stables demolished – the end of an era. Mulberry Court is on the right.

Early picture of The Boars Head circa 1920, showing the portico and the sign of Page's High Class Ales.

The White Bear about 1890. The driver of the cart has stopped for a drink. It was well-known that the horses were so used to stopping there they had to be whipped to pass it!

The last session in Royston Courthouse on 3rd October 1990. All the court officials came in early to pose for this historic picture. Harold Shaw, the former postmaster of Royston, consented to pose as the accused. Those present are: The magistrates: Mrs. B. E. M. Bowmer, Miss J. P. Etheridge (chairman) and Mrs. J. Johnson, Bassingbourn; David Barker, Solicitor, Clerk to the Justices; Man with documents, Eric Gentle; Policeman, P.C. David Turner; in the dock Harold Shaw; Crown Prosecutor, Mrs Sassoli; Defence Solicitor, Mr. T. Prestbury (Walkers).

This family of ''Macedonian'' gypsies was about to be escorted over the county boundary and eventually to the coast 1904.

Sergeant Pennicott and his son David, a police cadet. Sergeant Pennicott was Royston's police sergeant and lived in the police house next to the Police Station in Priory Lane. (Photo dated 1948.)

One of the cells in the old Police Station.

Below: The Resisters Sale of 1903 at Royston Police Station. When rates were not paid, t property of such "resisters" was distrained and sold.

The Parish Church before the tower restoration of 1872, taken from the gardens of Priory House.

Interior of the Mission Room, built in 1935 in Queens Road. This was run as a Sunday School and Mission Hall for the 'new' houses built near the station in the 19th century. Decorated on this occasion for Harvest Festival. During World War II this was used by Queens Road School for school dinners.

"His Eminence the Cardinal Archbishop of Westminster at Royston..."

The first Catholic church was in Serby Avenue and here we see Cardinal Bourne, Archbishop Westminster, arriving in Royston to open it in 1912.

105453

Catholic Church, Royston.

The second Catholic Church (Melbourn Road) showing its original architecture. Completed in 19 and dedicated to St. Thomas of Canterbury.

The Parish Church Choir about 1950

ck row: Sears, Jacklin, Bushell, Wick, Goode, Wick. *2nd row:* Rosendale, Not Known, Charter, ington, Bushell, J. Parker, C. Chalkley. *3rd row:* R. Gentle, C. Walters, P. Davies, D. King, F. Stair, Izzard, Charter, D. Sermon. *Front row:* F. Drake, H. Kemp, Sir Cecil Newman, Rev. Devonshire, Stanley Beale, Albert Gilbert, Harold Jellis, Guy Abrey.

is long building, near the entrance of the Offord tes, was used as a restaurant in the Priory rdens which were laid out as memorial gardens. . Shepherd the head gardener raised the plants the gardens in the greenhouse on the left of the picture.

This 1950 cartoon by 'Wink' is most appropriate here: the 'victim' Stanley Beale, for many years organist and choirmaster.

A lovely picture taken about 1935 of the grounds of Priory House and showing the old Priory po

An early picture of the Priory Gardens showing the fountain, probably mid 1950's.

These two postcards of the Cave in Melbourn Street dated 1910 show the carvings in relatively good condition. 85 years later deterioration has become so bad, many of the carvings are difficult to see.

Flooding occurs periodically in the Ca
This photo of 1965 shows two coun
workers doing their best in sme
conditions to clean up the mess. (Tak
from the W.I.'s 1965 scrapbook, which i
superb source of information, especially
that year, when they celebrated their Gol
Jubilee.

From *The Royston Crow* 1896.

14. MILITIA ENCAMPMENT. ROYSTON. 1904.
"ARRIVAL OF THE OLD HANDS" PUB. BY ROBERT H. CLARK.

A remarkable picture. 91 years ago (1904) there was a Militia Encampment on Royston Heath. The soldiers, known as the "Old Hands", who came by train, marching towards their camp. Of great interest are the spectators, especially the way they were dressed.

"On Parade" at the Militia Encampment of 1904 – all very splendid.

From the First World War. The postcard on the left was in full colour in its original form. Dated 1915.

Don't be Alarmed, the 4th Cheshires are on guard at Royston.

Below: is a picture of Queen's Road School, built in 1910 which was used as a Soldiers Hospital. Dated 1914. Casualties from France came over by boat and train

A Remembrance Day parade exact date unknown, possibly 1938. Older Roystonians will recognise many of the faces. Who was the boy so well turned out and marching so smartly?

November 1939. Remembrance Day Parade at Royston Parish Church, showing the St. John's Ambulance Brigade section.

Royston – Camp 29. Taken in Summer 1947. The camp was first built as a prison camp for Italian prisoners of war. It then became a German camp and the prisoners remained until the last prisoners were repatriated in February 1948. After they left, local people desperate for housing moved into the huts until they got permanent accommodation.

Italian prisoners of war. The prisoners lived at the camp on the Heath and worked at several locations in Royston and the surrounding area. The five prisoners shown were working at Greys, a farm at Therfield, owned by the Darling family.

Major Darling and senior district officers in the Home Guard 1940/42.
Back row: ?. Etheridge, Dr. Fox, Mark Hewitt, Capt. Jacklin, Sir Humphrey de Trafford
Front row: Col. Faure-Walker, Not Known, Major Darling, Not Known, Not Known.

The Royston Town Band became the Home Guard Band
Back row: Joe Stockbridge, ?. Smith, Not Known, Frank Simons, Joe Smith, George Beale,
"Gerry" Bradman
Front row: Jim Beale, Frank Greenhill (bandmaster), Capt. Jacklin, Sid Day.

Members of Royston Civil Defence (A.R.P.) in the early part of World War II.
Back row: Miss Mothersole, Alf Pepper, ?. Sheldrick, Flo Roker, F. Doughton,
Not Known, Frances Fuller.
Front row: ?. Harris, Lewyn Seeley, Dr. A. Skyrme, ?. Goddard, Harold Goddard.

Trowel Presentation.
Major General (USAF Retd.) Wray receives the trowel used in the cornerstone laying of the
USAF Memorial in Royston from R. J. Gavin, Mayor of Royston. The three gentlemen standing
between the General and the Mayor are G. Bedwell, F. J. Smith, G. Shakespeare.

An early picture of Royston Hospital staff and patients — all dressed up and ready for Christmas dinner.

Hospital Carnival 1924: The Royston Hospital Entry arranged by Miss E. Clarke "A Pack of Cards" won 1st prize in the Most Novel Entry Section. The participants were from very well known Royston families. *Spades:* Ace–Mrs. A. W. Deards, King–Mr. A. R. Thair, Queen–Mrs. W. E. Titchmarsh, Jack–Stanley Evans, Pages–L. Varney and Drayton. *Hearts:* Ace–Sister D. Clarke, King–Mr. A. O. R. Bishop, Queen–Nurse H. Tamplin. Jack–Clifford Humphris, Pages–Dick Mays and Lea Grundy. *Diamonds:* Ace–Mrs. Stanley Hoy, King–Mr. W. G. Bedwell, Queen– Mrs. A. R. Thair, Jack–J. Wiltshire, Pages–Peter and Dudley Hoy. *Clubs:* Ace–Mrs. J. B. Bishop, King–Mr. W. C. Titchmarsh, Queen–Mrs. A. O. R. Bishop., Jack–G. Bedwell,Pages–J. Bedwell and D. Bishop.

1928 Fete and Procession to raise funds for Royston Hospital. A very special year during which the new Children's Ward was opened by the Prince of Wales.

Presentation to Lady Joan Newman of miniature of "Sister of Order" Badge of the St. John's Ambulance Brigade (given by Royston Nursing division) by C.Supt. Mrs. Sparkes. On the right of the picture are Mrs. Mizen and Mrs . Bilk. On the left, Mrs. Rayner, Miss Hart and Mrs. Atkins. (c. 1959)

Royston Nursing Cadet Division of St. John's Ambulance in 1949, beautifully turned out. The were looked after and managed by Miss Hart, winning various trophies over the years *Back row:* June Jones, Lilian Oakman, Joyce Gavin, Sheila Young, Doreen Young, Kath Raymen Bessie Dellar, Janet Dinkle.
Front row: Shirley Marsom, Mary Pigg, Gwen Cowper, Miss Hart, Peggy Palmer, Audre Jellis, Beryl Smith.

The wedding portrait of Frederick Parrott and his wife Sarah in 1905.
A fine example of fashion at the time.

epresentatives from Women's Institutes from Royston and District off to Buckingham Palace in
1965, in celebration of their Golden Jubilee. They look really splendid.

RATCLIFFE   REID   SPENCER   TH

Dick Joice presenting the trophy to the winning Royston team in the Anglia TV Quiz betwe
Anglian towns 14th July 1964.

Franklin Engleman talks to Bob Clark in "Down Your Way" a popular radio programme,
running for many years. (1967)

Some of the men who worked at Royston Gas Company. (Photograph probably 1950's.)

Mr. Colton opening a retort at the Royston Gas Company Works in Mill road, which used to be known as Gas Works Lane. There were always small boys who came to fill buckets of water for Mr. Colton to damp down the hot coals. This was considered to be a great treat.

Royston Water Company Works on London Road. One of the most important developments in 19th century Royston. There are no springs or river at Royston so water had to be obtained by drilling through the chalk.

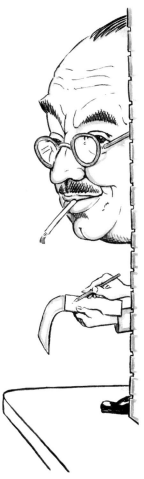

Left: Michael J. Cooke, owner of Warren Brothers and Cooke, and Publishers of The Royston Crow. A happy and generous man who died in 1994 and is sadly missed.

Right: Caricature of Arthur "Wink" Thair by himself. Arthur was a professional Ladies & Gents hairdresser with a salon in High Street. He loved Royston and its history and took great pleasure in drawing and painting caricatures of local people.

Bob (I) Bob (II) Bob (III)

ree generations of Robert H. Clark, Royston photographers and publishers of the famous series Royston postcards, much sought after by local collectors. The business is still operating under the 4th generation Clark – Colin.

e inhabitants of Hope cottages. This was a small row of cottages situated between the Town Hall d the present Police Station. The site is now part of the Health Centre gardens and part of the wn Hall car park. The original photo was taken in 1867 by Mr Latchmore Hitchin copied by ank Hinkins in 1891 and copied again by Cecil Rayner in 1985. Hence deterioration in quality but still a wonderful example of what all generations wore at that time, nearly 130 years ago.

Mr. George Beale outside his stonemason's premises in Melbourn Road, opposite the junction with Mill Road.before World War II when the railings were removed as part of the war effort. Now workshops of Ketteringhams soft furnishers.

58

Royston has a long tradition of pageantry, carnivals, processions etc, A. King, Saddler, on Market Hill, site of the present day Library, splendidly decorated for George Vs Coronation in 1911. Compare with photo of same shop in Volume I on page 24.

An interesting photograph in that it shows a band and platform on The Green, Kneesworth Street and this would have been part of the Hospital fund raising days in the 1920's.

ssembly for carnival on the corner of London Road and Barkway Street. The large house, called The Red House, has since been demolished.

bbot House, furniture shop of the Abbot family in High Street, decorated for George VI's Coronation in 1937.

This interesting and attractive looking house once stood on th corner of The Warren and Barkway Street. This is the site Joseph Leete's house, now an Old People's Home known as Lower Warren.

The ancient barn that stood between "The Boars Head" and Halstead & Kestell's shop on Market Hill, now the Home Improvement Centre.

ca 1950. On London Road. A
veloper bought this house and
plied for planning permission to
nolish it. The Georgian society
s one of many objectors, but the
s were removed, windows taken
t and eventually this fine house
s demolished and replaced with
two blocks of houses and flats.

This house at the Town Hall corner behind the
Town Hall was purchased and demolished to
make way for the temporary buildings used as
offices by the Town Hall staff, which are still used.

arden Lane, these 19th century cottages
re situated on the south side of Garden
Lane near the junction with The Warren.

Mr. Wilson the Blacksmith standing at the rear of
his forge, 3 Kneesworth Street, near the Cross. The
Wilson family were Blacksmiths at the Forge for
over 200 years. (c. 1930).

Above: Royston Laundry in Lower Gower Road, shown with staff and vehicles, in the mid 1960's, *l to r:* Don Sharpe, Arthur Bonner, Alex Walford, Bill Armstrong (manager) Peter King and Michael Wilmott.

Below: Early 17th century window from Wilson's Forge, 3 Kneesworth Street, demolished 1974. The window is now in Royston Museum.

The corner of Mill Road and The Green. These houses were demolished to make way for the present houses. They were famous for their lovely front gardens. "Banjo Billy" a famous Cambridge busker lived in the end cottage.

Old Cottages in Mackerel Hall, demolished to make way for Cedar Crescent.

The Lime Kiln Works on Barkway Road. A useful source of employment. Closed down about 1918 after a worker was killed from falling chalk.

An early road widening scheme in the centre of Royston in 1927. The scar that was left has never satisfactorily healed. This is the demolition of The Crown Hotel at the Cross. This actual photograph was used by local artist E. H. Whydale as inspiration for one of his better known etchings.

From *The Royston Crow* 1896.

Grade 1 listed building in Royston known as Thurnalls, in Melbourn Street, seen from the nave roof looking north. Former home of the Beldam family with the initials I.A.B. in the ironwork over the door. Next door is the Banyers, named after Rev. Edward Banyer, vicar of

One of the bedrooms in Thurnalls, 18 Melbourn Street, showing the painted ceiling and oak panelling shown here painted white but recently restored to its original condition.

decorative fireplace inside Thurnalls. An ~~~ustration of this is in Kingston's "History of Royston" from a painting by Mr. Thurnall.

Tanyard Drift in 1904, looking south, now called Tannery Drift

Stile Plantation, one of the pleasant walks in Royston linking Barkway Road with Newmar
Road. In the 19th century this, among others, was planted on the outskirts of the town, by lo
benefactors. The young boy at the bottom right hand corner makes this photo about 1900.